BLISS POETRY

by Robert E Bliss USMC (Ret)

RoseDog Books
PITTSBURGH, PENNSYLVANIA 15238

RoseDog Books
585 Alpha Drive, Suite 103
Pittsburgh, PA 15238
Visit our website at *www.rosedogbookstore.com*

ISBN: 979-8-89211-288-8
eISBN: 979-8-89211-786-9

DREAM WIND

Flowing
Under above
In the deep sleep of night
Somewhere beneath my pillow lover
I am lost in the tornado of a dream
The recurrent capture of lost love
Spins in the mind becoming wind-storm
Twisting there and here
High above the plain of consciousness
And spat out
Hard-scattered against the ground
Much too dizzy and shaken
To catch the equilibrium of the moment
And waking up in the middle of a dream
In the deep sleep of night

I AM PULLING IN MY ANCHORS NOW AND GIVE YOU YOUR FREEDOM FROM THESE MY UNCHARTED SEAS.

I AM PULLING IN MY ANCHORS NOW THAT HAVE GONE TO RUST TOO LONG BURIED IN THE SANDS OF YOUR HEART.

LIGHTHOUSE

I BESEECH, I BECKON,
I REACH OUT WITH MY FINGERS OF LIGHT.
I BRING YOU BACK
FROM YOUR FOG-WORN NIGHT.
I CARESS YOU WITH MY BEACON
IN YOUR LONELINESS.
I AM THE TRUTH IN YOUR DARKNESS.
I GIVE MEANING TO THE SEEKING
IN YOUR WATER-SOAKED HULLS.
I KISS YOUR SAILS WITH A HOMEWARD WIND,
AND GUIDE YOUR CHILDREN
WITH A GENTLE HAND.
THROUGH THE STORM,
MY HAND UPON THE WHEEL,
WITH YOU I STEER.
I PULL YOU IN AND TEMPER YOUR FEARS.
I AM THE WOMB IN YOUR DARKNESS.
I AM THE LIGHT.
I SEND YOU OUT AND TAKE YOU BACK AGAIN.
I AM YOURS IN THE NIGHT....

MOON DREAMS

An ancient moon shines down on this land
That we have known for fifteen years.
The earth mother has put her children to sleep
Where they dream in moon-glow
nestled in her nurturing hands.
Pines lift silver branches in a flirting wind
And dance a waltz of sadness
As if knowing that I am near.
In the brook the night frogs creep
Round stones washed smooth by memories.
In the woods an owl swoops down
On its unsuspecting prey
And for a moment
I am caught between wisdom and madness.
Somewhere a frightened creature cries out in the darkness
Too late I fear, too late.
The moon's gentle radiance leads my eye
To a broken old fence
with a gate that swings in silence.
In dream-time I see you on the other side
Your hair gold and flying in the night.
And just before I call your name
Clouds roll in
And you disappear from my sight.

GARDEN FLOWER

I stand before you
Universal and God-like,
Yet humble and afraid.

Through a long winter I have held your seed,
Protecting you and waiting.
Today I hold your gifts in my hands
And wonder...
What is the secret of your creation?
More lies here than a blending of the elements,
I am sure.

It is no matter,
I will pull your weeds
And love you with able fingers.

Sometimes,
Looking upon you,
Self absorbed,
I almost become you.
So close your essence becomes me.
How I wear you
Like a sweater
As these Catskill Mountains wear their clouds.

Inevitably,
When it is time for you to go
Into the long winter,
I will go too,
clutching your seeds
In hands made by the Gods
For planting....

FOR YOU!

From atop this barren mountain
So close against the sky
Clouds hug ancient boulders
Where eagles once did fly.

The mist below obscures the view
Of a hard and lonely climb
As I try to remember the beauty here
A world apart from time.

The valley below so beautiful then
The air so sweet and clear
But the wind is hard and troubled now
And blows against my fears.

A fire came and scorched this land
And burned all life away
Now all that's left are memories
Of flowers that bloomed in May.

A trail of ashes lies ahead
Across this mountain hell
And whether eagles will soar again
It's much to soon to tell.

Look out on the carnage here
The future seems so bleak
And in the wind are syllables
Of a name I used to speak.

The trail obscured and broken
There seems no path to take
Down from this lifeless landscape
Where love has made mistakes.

Wounded and exhausted
My blood upon the ground
It mixes with the ashes
And follows me around.

For I am just a man with needs
Who needed once more to see
This place we called our own one time
Where you once walked with me.

A moment here will last forever
But the past is just a dream
And as the sun goes gently down
I hear this mountain scream.

Nature takes it course they say
And nothing stays the same
And I will leave this mountain
Just the way I came.

I turn around and to the west
I see the Evening Star
Close enough to touch I think
Yet far away so far...

And that is where I'll find you now
When I need you for awhile
Out there where the eagles fly
Is where I'll find your smile.

I've never wanted much in life
As I've traveled through this land
Only love for love's sake
And to hold you by the hand.

In the woods I call your name
where the heart moves the stones in streams
birds in flight are calling there
your voice is what I hear
and everything I see and touch
everything I do
has a single meaning now
it's all for the love of you

In the yard the willow weeps
as snow comes gently down
the Christmas Time has come again
and people laugh in town
I look down empty streets for you
and wonder how you are
as distance takes its distant dance
my love still travels far

The road to love is long and far
and I've been such a fool
I've trampled on our sacred vows
and treated you so cruel
and now I die a thousand deaths
and realize what I've lost
this Winter of my sorrow
is colder than its frost

TO NANCY MY LOVE

In this house without you here
I walk from room to room
where silence screams from everywhere
yet much too loud to hear
In my heart without you near
an emptiness is all I feel
I search the evening sky for answers
and cry a thousand tears

I did not know I had hurt you so
and thought my love was just enough
to carry us from day to night
so little did I know
if only you had told me
if only I had known
for I'm afraid I've lost you now
and the moon has lost its light

I went to the mountains to look for you
and found myself instead
there was snow upon the frozen ground
and demons in my head
I came as close to God
as I ever will again
and burned my soul to save the man
the little that I found

I've searched a thousand dreams for you
in the darkness of my nights
and find you sometimes hiding there
before the morning light
I see you in our bedroom mirror
and turn to take your hand
but a shadow of you is all that's there
and you vanish from my sight

You have been my love and friend
the one I never meant to hurt
you opened my eyes to the beauty in life
and wrapped me in your skirts
and love that I had never had
you gave to me.. my wife
in my life a light you've been
and will be till the end

I pray that you are safe and well
and think of us sometimes
especially now at Christmas time
when you hear the Christmas bells
and when you see the lovely lights
upon the trees so tall
think of our beautiful family
the goodness in it all

Remember this my darling wife:
anything for you I'll do
everything and anything at all

SICK HOME

The wheelchair waits patiently its turn
In quiet metal-muscle repose,
In a room where idle illness and stagnant suffering
Shuffle upon the floor;
Where Gods give not a thought
To devine recovery.

The bed angel
Holds its human form in soft white wings,
But turns her head and looks away.

The flowers stand in front of a mirror
Reflecting unknown friends
Of certain uncertain situations;
Of broken dreams
That have found somewhere new
To gather moss again.

The walls grow greener and darker
Into another long and lonely night.
The flowers nod their heads
To the black linoleum floor,
Where the ancient broken spider
Crawls around unnatural antiseptic wonders,
And into a jar of oblivion
Where it screws itself to the lid.

THE FROZEN MOON

Remember when we talked about that old frozen moon
And the climb up its mountains;
The struggle so hard,
The peak too soon.
Remember those days when the war ran on
And me standing on another man's legs...
We sat by the river drinking beer
And eating hard-boiled eggs.
Do you remember those talks about space
While men walked on that cold, cold moon...
We went fishing for sharks
Catching trout with spoons.
We'd lay in the grass
Conjuring up smoke dreams
About new loves to come,
The Sea Of Tranquillity and moon beams.
The tree's flowers fell on our faces.
We were there but in different places.
Remember what happened at the Cape Of May
Under the new frozen moon;
We drank too much and made a scene
And didn't care what the people might say.
We reached out across that old frozen moon,
And laughing we held each other like bothers,
Two guitars playing the same tune.
Seems like yesterday when that music played,

And even though we've grown older
And gone our separate ways,
That wonderful old moon
Just stays and stays....

REFLECTION

It was placed on a shelf in a room.
Cold and dark like a tomb.
Abandoned to the years
To silence shadows and gloom
Where voices once laughed
And music played
Now only memories loomed.

It was left there needed no more.
Left to gather dust facing a door
That would no longer open
As it had before.
Left there with spiders
To spider the floor.

Left among books where the poets knew well
That love is magic the sorcerers spell.
But in that room
Where specters dwell
Our love was left leaning
Where it tottered and fell...

THE BEST OF BAD HEMINGWAY

He was an old man now and the years of work in the fields showed in his weathered face and swollen hands, but his eyes were clear and blue like the water in the Caribbean. Although wounds earned in the Spanish War kept him in great pain he never complained and went about his work with determination and pride.

In the coolness of the evening the children would follow him out of the village to a large rock near the coconut palms where the sand reaches the sea. He told his stories to them with innocence and guilt like when you kill your first deer or take your first trout and knowing what death means. He told them stories about the sea and the great proud fish that lived there that could not be killed by the fishermen because they were too smart for the baited hook and would live on long after the men in boats were gone. The children loved the old man's stories and would listen to him until the sun sank into the sea, and at night in their beds his stories would become their dreams.

The old man's days took on the uniformity of the tides. When the tide was out he would work in the fields, and when it was in he would take his boat out with the others to fish for whatever the sea would give them. "Soon," he told his friend, Pablo, "I will not have the strength to work the land, and the sea will no longer accept me because I will grow feeble and stupid." Pablo would laugh good-naturedly at his friend and tell him, "Juan, the sea will have you for many seasons to come, my friend." It was wonderful to laugh with his friend, but the old man knew his time was growing short and nothing could be done about it.

Everything was the same to him now in his old ways. Everything except death, which would be new to him and would surely embrace him like a man embraces a woman for the first time and never wanting to let go. "At least," he thought, "death is something that can be relied on, and when it comes it never leaves you." And because it was much older than him, even older than the sea, he was sure he could show it the respect it deserved.

In his small boat the old man and Pablo fished the churning sea in the hot afternoon sun. On the beach the little children played and watched the boats bobbing up and down, in and out of sight, while the big gulls fought over bits of chum bait in the blue water. The old man let the sun wash his brown wrinkled face as he held the fishing line in his scarred hands and let the motion of the sea rock him back and forth between his dreams.

Once the old man had been in love with a beautiful woman from the village on the other side of the Island. He remembered how her hips swayed like the early morning waves as she walked along the beach and how her hair moved in a gentle wind and her eyes were the color of the mountains in the afternoon. She had drowned in an accident at sea many years ago but her closeness to him, even now, gave him strength and perspective. As he rolled with the sea in a half sleep the old man thought he heard her calling him from the beach. "Juan, Juan, come home." He looked up suddenly to see the gulls flying near the boat and crying to each other in the wind.

He lay back against the bulkhead squinting his eyes into the setting sun and realized he had no regrets now near the end. He had given and he had taken in equal amounts. The old man sat there holding a line that reached from his soul into the clear blue sea. Memories of his youth came back to him. And he remembered the war, and the passion of honest love, and he knew what it must be like when a long hot Summer becomes Winter and stays with you forever...

OFFER THE STARS

I offer the stars yet you turn away
I need your touch but you will not stay
A shadowed woman and a lonely man
When life is hard you do what you can

Yet I believe fate will change this course
There's much to respect in its gentle force
Only time binds the hands that reach for more
Where the days may find a friendly shore

Come along and Share my tasty tea
So many things I need you to see
The hour grows late as we take the ride
Our dreams are spinning and often collide

Reach far enough and you'll touch the moon
And all that is hoped for will be with you soon
Walk with courage whatever you choose
And she'll change your destiny with nothing to lose

THE GIFT OF LOVE

A person both gentle and also kind
She stays with those who leave us behind
There are so few people who do this thing
Holding the hands of those souls to sing

While Tears of Love float in the air
Whenever Jennifer is with them there
Bringing peace of mind to families all
A life worth living and the last joyful call

To praise such a gift so divine to know
The love in her heart continues to grow
Walking with the Gods both day and night
Gifted grace always brings what is right

The light in her eyes so bright and serene
Follows her through life wherever she's been
She flows like a butterfly high on the air
Dominance of spirit is there to share

I'm happy to know this person my friend
And I'll cherish her forever until the end
For she walks with angels into each life
And gathers their treasures, troubles and strife

THE GIFT OF FLOWERS

Flowers from the gardens of Nature's soul
Beautifully unbounded wherever you stroll
Color unimaginable at every turn
The wisdom of its creation I want to earn

God invented flowers at the top of His game
And nothing so creative has been the same
I look into an Orchid and a universe appears
And find a world that diminishes my fears

Created I feel for our retrospection
And worth every moment of our inspection
Life can be difficult to measure the task
Yet flowers want nothing nor do they ask

Put on this earth to make us feel good
Giving us hope yet don't know they should
A flower is a gift from the heavens aloft
Wondrous colors from God's gentle cough

When everything else tries to break me down
I search the skies then look at the ground
It's there I find what I'm looking for
And all I need do is step outside my door

SHADOW LIGHT

Out in the forest you'll find Shadow Light
Light through the trees an unusual sight
A beautiful vision of calm and deflection
As Nature points to a perfect direction

The angle of the sun will change all day
Creating illusions dreamlike in every way
Softly in summer and dramatic each fall
All the better when her trees are tall

Softness personified from top to ground
With a breeze in the leaves much better found
Yet even more striking in the absence of sound
Experienced once and you'll stay around

Taken for granted unless wisdom prevails
Much is missed and what it entails
Follow your heart as you walk in the woods
And life will just happen as it always should.

CHRISTMAS TIME

The Christmas time is in the air
With Holiday greetings and gifts to share
The green and red so pleasantly near
Where Family and Friends share Seasonal cheer

The children dream of one perfect night
And a star in Bethlehem finds a holy sight
The magic surrounds us in our winters lairs
Gifts and greetings pile up on the stairs

Happiness and gladness spreads like the flu
I look for the mistletoe and stand next to you
For you are my Xmas in all that you do
Life is excited with everything new

Trees in the homes and wreaths on doors
Life renewed where the future holds more
A time for all who step into the light
To remember the animals wild in the night

And maybe the world will be better for this
With peace and love and a gentle kiss
If only Christmas were here every day
With no hungry children only time to play.

CLOUDS

Oh thé clouds drifting against the sky
Always they catch my discerning eye
To sail away with them my hearts desire
And steal me away from internal fires

Come gather me up and take me away
On wings of freedom for I shall not stay
One life abandoned and another one new
And all of this I would share with you

Pillows of white slide into my sight
They gather me up and hold me tight
And push me along into the night
Comfort and peace and everything right

Feelings sublime as I circle the blue
I search these heavens and look for you
Alone in my thoughts I need you near
Come fly with me there's nothing to fear

A home in these clouds so perfect and fine
I need your love to make them mine
Sail away from the madness far below
For you this and more I shall bestow.

MY MOTHER

Landscapes of nature devine and sincere
Expressions of beauty ever so near
Like strolling through a kaleidoscope heavenly made
Where the songs of life are musically played

Colors of Glory stand up and shout
And calm the emotions as you walk about
An amusement park of joy every day
Gather your thoughts for you'll want to stay

Waterfalls of white tumbling into the sea
Where the land expands so open and free
Flowers lift heads and reach for the sun
Such brilliance and beauty in everyone

Rocks in the streams washed soft and clean
Visit the Mother and you'll see what I mean
She freely walks right into our hearts
And opens our souls to Her healing arts

Snow-capped mountains stand guard at their post
Offering strength and courage for what's needed most
Wilderness opens across the world
And a Godly wonder rolls out unfurled

Pines stand tall like medieval knights

Watching over the kingdom protecting Her rights
A solemn church is the Mother's throne
Where Her seeds of love are gently blown

A place where I always want to be
To lie in Her meadows and climb Her trees
Nothing in this world could make me leave
For I am Her son and in Her I believe

A WORLD TOO MUCH

A world against us in time and space
Frightens the mind and quickens the pace
Tempers that fly not enough released
Hostilities so many too little peace

Demands take us away from who we are
The distance to enlightenment so very far
The world is changing and not for the good
So much confusion little understood

Generations of mistakes bury us down
While war and attrition follow us around
So much beauty dissolves into hate
Time against us are we too late

Minds polluted as are the lakes
How do we recover from these mistakes
I look to the mountains and pray for hope
Yet we slide and fall on earthly slopes

The world too much with us in every way
Changes are wanting If we should stay
Only love for each other will save the day
And the care of our planet where the children play

Contents

FOREWORD

The rapid progress in technology makes it extremely important to know all about the new technological advancements that occur in this world. Becuase if we aren't update in this world, we will be left behind and will eventually forgotten by everyone. So it is important to stay update.

The book "Unmanned Aerial Vehicles " edited by myself provides a number of chapters regarding these aerial vehicles or drones. This book many covers the definition, working and importance of drones of real life

The contributions of several countries in making the drones and latest technologies have also been taken into account to help readers stay updated.

PREFACE

I myself was interested in making drones from a very young age but due to some financial and family issues i couldn't achieve my goals. So i thought to combine all the information i knew about the drones so that other children who wannna achieve this goal will find no difficulty in doing so. I hope this book will serve as a perfect guide to them.

I

Introduction

Technological advancements has impacted social, economical and personal life from business approaches to international wars. These transformations can be also benefitted by these advancements.

Unmanned Aerial Vehicles (UAVs) also known as remotely operated aircrats are the best examples of this change. These vehicles don't need any human onboard which is what makes them different from manually monitored aircrafts and can be autonomously operated from the ground control or through remote control.

These are a part of integrated Unmanned Aerial vehicle system which includes communication link the radio station and the ground control. We will talk about these things later in the book

Perhaps in 1916 the first Semi - Automatic Airplane was developed which was named as Aerial Torpedoes. The Royal Navy started to use in 1933 for the shooting practices. Later on with the advent and integration of advanced navigation sensors UAV became a part of defence forces. The emergence of technology not only removed the limitations of UAVs nut also expanded their uses in the commercial background from agriculture, to law and ordrer monitoring, delivery serveices etc.

The term drone was being used since many days in early days of aviation which only applied to remotely flown aircrafts used for the shooting practices in the battleships like the 1920s Fairy Queen and the 1930s de Haviland Queen Bee. The later examples include Airspeed Queen Wasps and the Miles Queen marinet used as replacement by GAF Jindvik

On addition to the software, the autonomous drones also employ a host of advanced technologies that allow them to carry out difficult missions without human interventions. This includes, cloud computing, computer learning, alrtificial learning, deep machine learning etc.

<u>Unmanned Aerial Vehicles</u> is defined as " powered, aerial vehicles that doesn't carry a human operator and uses aerodynamic forces to provide vehicle lift , can fly autonomously, or be piloted remotely, can be expandable or recoverable and can carry a lethal or non- lethal payload." However missiles with warheads are not considered UAVs because the vehicle itself is the munition. Also the relation of UAVs to remote controlled aircrafts in unclear , UAVs may or may not include remote controlled aircrafts.

The term **unmanned aircraft system (UAS)** adopted by the United States Department of Defense and the United States Federal Aviation Adminstration in 2005 according to their **Unmanned Aerial Vehicle Roadmap 2005 -2030.**

The International Civil Aviation Organization (ICAIO) and the British Civil Aviation Authority adopted this term, also used in European Union's Single - European Sky (SES) Air - Traffic Management (ATM) Reasearch (SESAR Joint Undertaking) 2020 . The term ephasizes the importance of elements other than the aircrafts . It includes systems like ground control, data link, and other support system.

A similar term for the Unmanned Aerial Vehcile is **Remotely Piloted Aircrafts (RPAs)**

Enter Caption

Predator MQ 1 Drone

UAVs are descended from target drones and remotely piloted vehicles (RPVs) employed by the military forces of many countries in the decades immidiately after World War - 2. Modern UAVs debuted as an important weapon system in 1980s when the Israeli Defence Forces fitted small drones resembling large model airplanes with trainable television and infrared cameras with target designators for laser - guided munitions , downlinked to a control station. Rendered undectatable ny small sizes and quiet engines , these vehicles proved effective in the battlefield. Other Armed Forces learned from the experiment probably the US Army and they started to use the drones the force.

II
The Military Aircrafts

Apache - 64 Helicopters

Airbus military aircraft

Aircrafts have been a fundamental part of military power from the 20th Century. Generally speaking, all military aircrafts fall into the following categories :-

1. **<u>The fighter aircrafts</u>** - The ones that secure the border and are armed with missiles. These are used to chase enemy aircrafts , bombers and helicopters. These are also used to control essential airspaces also. These are also used to target ground targets, surviellance, attack aircrafts etc.
2. **<u>Bomber Aircrafts</u>** - These are used to drop bombs on troops formations, grounded aircrafts, tanks, military establishments.
3. **<u>Helicopters</u>** - These are aircrafts that have rotary wings attatched to them. These are used to support ground troops, chase enemy aircrafts not basically attacking them , assualt enemy troops and for surviellance.

III

The History Of Aircrafts

When the first Practical aircrafts were produced in the form of Hot - Air Baloons and Hydrogen Baloons , in 1783 they were adopted quickly for militray duties.

In the 1793 , the French National Convention authorized the formation of a military tethered baloon organisation and a company of "Aerostiser" was formed on April 2 , 1794.

Two months later, the first military reconnaisance from such baloon was made around the city of Maubeuge. Until the Aerostisers were disbanded in 1799, there reports contributed to the success of French Armies in many battles and seiges.

True milittary aviation began with the perfection of navigable airships in the late 19th entury and the airplane in the first decade of 20th Century.

The wright brothers Wilbur and Orville Wright , who made the first powered, sustained and controlled flights in an airplane on December 17th 1903, belived such an aircraft would be useful mainly for military surviellance purposes. When they received the first contract of a Military aircraft from the U.S Government , in February 1908, it was a two - seater aircrafts at a speed of at least 40 miles (65 kmph) for a distance of 125 miles (200 km) . The Aircraft they deliverd in June 1909 was termed as " Airplane No.1 , Heavier than air Division , United States aerial fleet".

Man-made airship in the sky

The most formidable aircrafts of the years before World War 1 were airships rather than the airplanes. These were large self propelled aircrafts, consisiting of rigid metal frabic frame within which gas bags were filled which contains gases lighter than the hydrogen which helped the airships to stay in the air. The most ambitious aircrafts of this type was created by Ferdinand , Count von Zepplin which is currently shown in the picture. A typical zepplin could carry bombs of maximum weighing 50 Kgs each and

20 -2.5 kgs each incidenary bombs when most military airplanes were in the developement stage without any form of weapons and were just used for air - surviellance purposes.

Experiments with arming airplanes were made spasmodically 1910 when August Euler took out a German patent on machine gun installation . Bombing techniques were involved simultaneously. Dummy bombs were dropped on a target in the form of ship by the American Designer Glenn Curtis on June 30 , 1910 . This test was followed by the dropping of real bomb and the devising the first bomb sight. In England the Royal Flying Corps (RFC) fitted some of its aircrafts with bomb carriers , which consisted of bomb pipe rack besides the observer in the cockpit with small bombs retained by a pin. The pin was pulled over a target. The Naval wing of RFC attempted to drop torpaedos from airplanes with some success , and efforts were soon underway to discover some way to recover such crafts on ship board. In 1910, a Curtiss Biplane had been flown from and onto wooden platforms erected over the decks of the anchored U.S. Navy cruise ships and in May 1912 a pilot of the Naval Wing , RFC, flew a short S27 biplane from HMS Hibernia while the ship was at 10.5 knots.

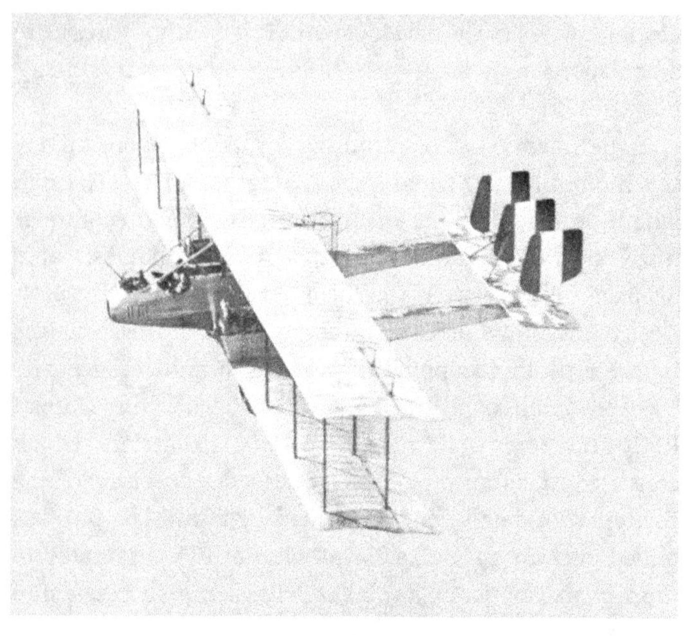

IV
The History of Drones

In the previous chapter we have seen how the humans began flying and types of aircrafts built and what were they used for.

In this chapter we will now begin with the history of drones. So we have divided the chapter into two parts : - 1. The Post war History

2. The Modern Day UAVs

Post War Period

After World War - II developments continued in vehicles developed previously like the American JB4 (using the telivision / radio guidance) , the **Austrailian GAF Jindivik** and the **Teledyne Ryan Firebee - 1** of 1951 while the companies like Beechcraft offered their **model 1001** for the U.S Navy in 1955 . Nevertheless, they were more or less similar to remotely controlled aircrafts until the Vietnam War.

In 1959 U.S Airforce was concerned about losing the pilots and their fleets in enemy territories , began planning of an uncrewed aircrafts. Planning intensified after Russia shot its U-2 Bomber in 1960. Within days, a highly classified UAV programme was started under the code name " Red Wagon " . The clash in 1964 August near Tonkin Gulf spearheaded the programme and three UAVs were devloped namely the **Ryan Model 147 , Ryan AQM - 91 and Lockheed D - 21** and used them in the first combat missions of the Vietnam war. When the Chinese Government showed the photos of shot down U.S UAVs the American Government had "no comments".

In 1973 in the Yop Kimpur War , Israel used UAVs as decoys to force the enemies to spend on expensive missiles After the 1973 war, few people from the team that developed this early UAV joined a small startup organization, that aimed to develope UAVs into a commercial product , eventually purchased by Tadiran which lead to the developement of first Israeli UAV

The Modern Day UAVs

UAVs are also in modern day life for various purposes. They were also used in the NASA missions. The Dragonfly spacecraft is being developed and is aimed at reaching Saturn's moon Titan. Its priary goal is to roam aroud the surface which will expand the areas sighted by The Landers. As a UAV, Dragonfly allows examination of potentially diverse soil. The drone is set to be launched in the year 2027 , and is estimated to take seven more years to reach Saturn

V

Classification of UAVs

The UAVs are not a single object, they also have various uses and in different fields. So they have been classified to be able to identify them easily. So the categories are as follows :-

1. **<u>Division based on aerodynamics</u>** - A variety of UAV systems have been developed and in the advancement phases includes The Fixed Wing Aircraft chopper, multi - copters, , motor parachute, and glider , UAV with Vertical Takeoff and Landing, congregrating ready - made parts

2. **<u>Division based on Landing</u>** - There are different landing and takeoff mechanisms used in drones. The two main mechanisms are**The Horizontal Takeoff and Landing (HTOL) and The Vertical Takeoff and landing (VTOL)** . HTOLs are considered as expansion of fixed- wing aircrafts. They have high cruise speeds and a smooth

landing. VTOLs are expert in flying , landing and hovering vertically , but they are limited by cruise speeds because of the slowing down of properllers

VI

The Components of a drone

The UAV is not a single system. There are various other systems that make a complete UAV. So, the components of a UAV are as follows :-

1. **Quadcopter Frame** - This is a structure (frame) in which all the other parts fit. It functions as a skeleton, with various components arranged in such a way that the drone's center of gravity is evenly distributed. Different drone frame structures are used for different drone designs, with a minimum of three propeller fitting gaps. They come in a variety of shapes and sizes.

2. **Motors** - Motors are essential for the propeller's rotation. This enhances the thrust force forpropelling the drone. The number of motors should, however, be equal to the number of propellers. The drone motors are also mounted in such a way that the controller can easily rotate them. Their rotation improves the direction

control of the drone. For the drone's efficiency, selecting the right motor is critical. Various parameters, such as voltage and current, thrust and thrust-to-weight ratio, power, efficiency, and speed, must all be carefully examined

3. **Electronic Speed Controllers** - This is an electronic control board that varies the motor's speed. It also acts as a dynamic brake. Thecomponent supports the ground pilot in estimating the drone's height while in flight. This is achieved by calculating the total amount of power consumed by all of the motors. The loss of power from the power reservoirs is linked to altitude.

4. **Flight Controller Boards** - The drone's takeoff location is recorded on the flight board in case the drone must return to itstakeoff location without being guided. This is known as the 'return to home' feature. It also determines and calculates the drone's altitude for the amount of power it consumes.Most commonly used fight controller boards:- a) Openpilot CC3D Flight Controller b) APM 2.8 Flight controller board c) KK 2.1.5 Multi-Rotor LCD Flight Control Board

5. **Propellers** - Propellers are clove-like blades structured to create a difference in air pressure. They cut through the air when in motion, creating a pressure difference between the top and bottom of the rotors. Low pressure on the top side compared to the bottom side causes the drone to lift into the air

6. **Radio Transmitter** - It is a channeled transmitter and a communicator to the drone. Each channel has a specific frequency capable of steering the drone in a certain motion. Drones require at least 4 channels for effective operation.

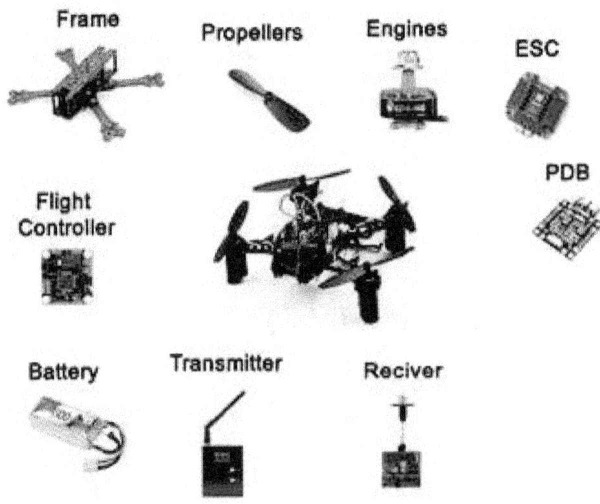

Basic Components of a Drone

VII

How Does A Drone Work

1. **Radar Positioning & Return Home** - The latest drones have dual Global Navigational Satellite Systems (GNSS) such as GPS and GLONASS.Drones can fly in both GNSS and non satellite modes. For example, DJI drones can fly inP-Mode (GPS & GLONASS) or ATTI mode, which doesn't use GPS.Highly accurate drone navigation is very important when flying, especially in drone applications such as creating 3D maps, surveying landscape and SAR (Search & Rescue) missions.When the quadcopter is first switched on, it searches and detects GNSS satellites. High end GNSS systems use Satellite Constellation technology. Basically, a satellite constellation is a group of satellites working together giving coordinated coverage and are synchronized, so that they overlap well in coverage. Pass or coverage is the period in which a satellite is visible above the local

horizon.

2. **UAV Drone GNSS On Ground Station Remote Controller** - The radar technology will signal the following on the remote controller display: -

- Signal that enough drone GNSS satellites have been detected and the drone is ready to fly
- Display the current position and location of the drone in relation to the pilot
- Record the home point for 'Return To Home' safety feature
- Pilot initiated return to home by pressing button on Remote Controller or in an app
- A low battery level, where the UAV will fly automatically back to the home point
- Loss of contact between the UAV and Remote Controller, with the UAV flying backautomatically to its home point

3. **Obstacle Detection And Collision Avoidance Technology** - The latest high tech drones are now equipped with collision avoidance systems. These use obstacle detection sensors to scan the surroundings, while software algorithms and SLAM technology produce the images into 3D maps allowing the drone to sense and avoid.

These systems fuse one or more of the following sensors to sense and avoid : -

- Vision Sensor
- Ultrasonic
- Infrared
- Time of Flight (ToF)
- Monocular Vision

The DJI Mavic 2 Pro and Mavic 2 Zoom have obstacle sensing on all 6 sides. The Mavic 2 uses both Vision and Infrared sensors fused into a vision system known as omnidirectional Obstacle Sensing.The DJI Mavic 2 obstacle sensing system is top drone technology. The Mavic 2 will sense objects, then fly around obstacles in front. It can do the same when flying backwards. Or hover if it is not possible to fly around the obstacle.This technology is known as APAS (Advanced Pilot Assistance System) on the DJI Mavic 2 and Mavic Air drones.In December 2019, the Skydio 2 drone was released. This also has obstacle avoidance on all sides.The Skydio 2 autonomy technology visualizes and calculates what's happening aroundthe drone. It can then intelligently predict what will happen next and will make accurate decisions multiple times a second.

4. Gyroscope Stabilization, IMU And Flight Controllers - Gyro stabilization technology give the UAV drone its smooth flight capabilities.The gyroscope works almost instantly to the forces moving against the drone, keeping it flying or hovering very smoothly. The gyroscope provides essential navigational information to the central flight controller.The inertial measurement unit (IMU) works by detecting the current rate of acceleration using one or more accelerometers. The IMU detects changes in rotational attributes like pitch, roll and yaw using one or more gyroscopes. Some IMU include a magnetometer to assist with calibration against orientation drift

5. **UAV Drone Propulsion Technology** - The propulsion system (motors, electronic speed controllers and propellers) are the drone technology, which move the UAV into the air and to fly in any direction or hover. On a quadcopter, the motors and propellers work in pairs with 2 motors /

propellers rotating clockwise (CW Propellers) and 2 motors rotating Counter Clockwise (CCW Propellers).They receive data from the flight controller and the electronic speed controllers (ESC) on the drone motor direction to either fly or hover. The Electronic Speed Controllers signal to the drone motors information on speed, braking and also provide monitoring and fault tolerance on the drone motors

6. **Realtime Telemetry Flight Parameters** - Nearly all drones have a Ground Station Controller (GSC) or a smartphone app, allowing you to fly the drone and to keep track of the current flight telemetry. Telemetry data showing on the remote controller many include UAV range, height, speed, GNSS strength, remaining battery power and warnings.Many UAV drone ground controllers use FPV (First Person View), which transmit the video from the drone to the controller or mobile device.

7. **No Fly Zone Drone Technology** - In order to increase flight safety and prevent accidents in restricted areas, the latestdrones from DJI and other manufacturers include a "No Fly Zone" feature.These are regulated and categorized by the Federal Aviation Authority (FAA). Manufacturers can change the no fly zone drone technology using UAV firmware updates.

8.

• 22 •

1.

VIII

Major Developements in the field - advanced versions of drones

The MQ - 1 Predator drone

First flew in 1994 and entered service the following year. The Predator, with a length of 26 feet 8 inches (8 metres) and a wingspan of 41 feet 8 inches (12.5 metres), is powered by a piston engine driving a pusher propeller. It flies at 80 miles (130 km) per hour and has an endurance of 24 hours. In addition to visible and infrared television, it carries synthetic aperture radar and passive electronic sensors, and it can also carry antitank missiles. Control inputs and sensor outputs are transmitted via communications satellite. A larger, turboprop-powered derivative of the Predator, the MQ-9 Reaper, has improved performance and carries a larger ordnance load. Both the Predator and the

Reaper have been used in the conflicts in Iraq and Afghanistan and have been purchased by allies of the United States.

U.S RQ-4 Drones

The most important of these is the U.S. RQ-4 Global Hawk, a jet-powered craft 44 feet (13 metres) long and with a wingspan of 116 feet (35 metres). The Global Hawk has a cruise speed of 400 miles (640 km) per hour and an endurance of some 36 hours, and it carries a variety of photographic, radar, and electronic sensors

The dragonfly

The Dragonfly spacecraft is being developed, and is aiming to reach and examine Saturn's moon Titan. Its primary goal is to roam around the surface, expanding the amount of area to be researched previously seen by Landers. As a UAV, Dragonfly allows examination of potentially diverse types of soil. The drone is set to launch in 2027, and is estimated to take a seven more years to reach the Saturnian system.

IX

Uses of Drone in Modern Day Life

In recent years, autonomous drones have begun to transform various application areas as they can fly beyond visual line of sight while maximizing production, reducing costs and risks, ensuring site safety, security and regulatory compliance and protecting the human workforce in times of a pandemic. They can also be used for consumer-related missions like package delivery, as demonstrated by Amazon Prime Air, and critical deliveries of health supplies.There are numerous civilian, commercial, military, and aerospace applications for UAVs. These include:

1. **General** - Recreation, Disaster relief, archeology, conservation of biodiversity and habitat, lawenforcement, crime, and terrorism.

2. **Commercial** - Aerial surveillance, filmmaking, journalism, scientific research, surveying, cargotransport, mining, manufacturing, Forestry, solar farming, thermal energy, ports and agriculture.

3. **Warfare** - As of 2020, seventeen countries have armed UAVs, and more than 100 countries use UAVs in a military capacity.The global military UAV market is dominated by companies based in the United States, Turkey China, Israel and Iran. By sale numbers, the US held over 60% military-market share in 2017. Top military UAV manufactures areincluding General Atomics, Lockheed Martin, Northrop Grumman, Boeing, Baykar, TAI, IAIO, CASC and CAIG. China has established andexpanded its presence in military UAV market since 2010. Turkey also established and expanded its presence in military UAV market. Of the 18 countries that are known to have received military drones between 2010 to 2019, the top 12 all purchased their drones from China. According to a report of 2015, Israeli companies mainly focus on small surveillance UAV systems and by quantity of drones, Israel exported 60.7% (2014) of UAV on the market while the United States export 23.9% (2014). Between 2010 and 2014, there were 439 drones exchanged compared to 322 in the five years previous to that, among these only small fraction of overall trade – just 11 (2.5%) of the 439 are armed drones. The US alone operated over 9,000 military UAVs in 2014; among them more than 7000 are RQ-11 Raven miniature UAVs.[122] General Atomics is the dominant manufacturer with the Global Hawk and Predator/Mariner systems productline.

CONCLUSION

The future generation is dependent on drones; they will create a new market. Drones are being upgraded and adopted by almost all commercial markets including precision agriculture, logistics and infrastructures. Future technology focused on increasing endurance, payload, improvement in the interaction between human and UAV and making clear rules and regulations for the safe and secure operation of UAV. Besides this, Integration of Artificial intelligence with drone technology will enable the drone to take decisions and independence to human controllers.